GET SMART ABOUT

ALBERT
EINSTEIN

Rocket Books

ADAM KENT

Get Smart about Albert Einstein
by Adam Kent

Published by Rocket Books, Inc.
New York, NY, USA

For kids...
who dream big,
who work hard to become better,
who get up when they fall,
who know we are all human and
all worthy of respect and success.

For my son Little Adam,
who lights up my life.

May your dreams come true.

This book is for you.

ADAM KENT

ABOUT THIS BOOK

This biography book is meant to be a fun, brief and inspirational look at the life of a famous person. Reading biographies can help learn from people who have experienced extraordinary things. While you read through the books in this series, think about how their experiences can help you in your own life!

As you read this book you will find bolded words. There are definitions of the words at the end of each page. You will also find interesting facts at the end of each chapter. Plus, there are some questions to get you thinking at the end of the book.

I hope you enjoy learning about this extraordinary person!

Have a great time reading,

Adam Kent

CONTENTS

GL

SE

GET SMART ABOUT

ALBERT

EINSTEIN

Rocket Books

ADAM KENT

ALBERT EINSTEIN
AT A GLANCE

Albert Einstein was one of the most famous physicists ever to live. He was also famous for being a genius with a high IQ. Throughout his life he developed important theories that changed our understanding of the universe. Some of his more notable contributions include the theory of relativity and $E = mc^2$. Einstein's work continues to influence scientific theory and his accomplishments continue to inspire people around the world. So, get ready to be inspired by and get smart about the one and only Einstein!

ALBERT EINSTEIN
FAST FACTS

1. Albert Einstein was born in the 1800s. Specifically, he was born March 14, 1879.

2. Einstein was born in Germany, which at the time was known as the German Empire.

3. He stopped high school early in order to avoid military service, but later finished his education receiving a doctorate, which is also known as a PhD.

4. Einstein won a Nobel Prize, which is one of the highest awards a scientist can win.

5. Albert Einstein had three children.

CHAPTER 1

THE EARLY DAYS

Albert Einstein was born on March 14, 1879. He was born in Europe, in Germany, in a town called Ulm. At the time, the place Einstein was born was actually called the German Empire, but today it is known as Germany.

Einstein grew up with his mother, father and one sister named Maja. Maja was two years older than Einstein. The family was Jewish, but they did not practice their religion much. This is an important fact that **influenced** him in the years following his birth as you will learn.

Einstein's father was a salesman and an engineer. His name was Hermann Einstein. He, along with his brother, Einstein's uncle, founded a company in Germany that sold electrical equipment. Einstein's mother's name was Pauline Koch. Pauline worked as a stay-at-home mother who looked after the household and raised Einstein and his sister Maja.

From a young age, Einstein

---

influence /ˈin-ˌflü-ən(t)s/ noun: the power to cause an effect in an indirect way verb: to affect or change indirectly *<example: His teacher influenced him.>*

was very curious. One of the first stories about his curiosity with the scientific unknown happened when he was just five. Einstein saw a compass for the first time. His father showed him one. Do you know what a compass is? Einstein was **fascinated** by the compass and wondered how it worked. This sparked in him a curiosity about unknown forces!

As a young boy, Einstein had what people considered to be speech difficulties. He also was passionate about playing the violin. He loved classical music too. This love stayed with him throughout his life.

---

fascinate /ˈfa-sə-ˌnāt/ verb: to hold the interest of in a powerful way *<example: The acrobat's performance fascinated her.>*

For elementary school. Einstein went to a school in Munich, Germany. It was called Luitpold Gymnasium. He never really felt that he fit in at the school. He also struggled with the school's strict educational style. He preferred more freedom to focus on the subjects that most interested him, like math and physics. His grade school experience was just okay.

Most of the experiences that influenced who Einstein would become took place outside of school. When Einstein was young, the family had a weekly guest at the house for lunch. This was a Jewish tradition. The guest was a boy named Max Talmud. Max was a Polish medical student. He became a bit of an informal tutor to Einstein for about five years.

Each week he gave Einstein new books and lessons on the topics that introduced him. He introduced Einstein to math, philosophy and science and really helped build his interest in those subjects. Einstein was so bright and captivated by what he was learning that he sped through books that would have taken people much older years to learn. Max was truly impressed. After a few years of tutoring him, Einstein matched Max's level of knowledge on the subjects he taught.

During this time, Max had given Einstein books that stayed in his mind even as he grew older. Once Max gave him a book to read on geometry, which Einstein called his "**sacred**[*] little book on geometry." He also gave him a children's science book series that would have a great impact on him. The series was released in 1867 by an author named Aaron Berstein. The title of the series was "Books on Physical Science." The book was written in German.

"Books on Physical Science" explored subjects such as light, distance, astronomy and meteorology. In one section, the author Berstein described what he imagined what a light wave would look like if you were to ride alongside it. This imagination inspired young Einstein. In fact, it

[*]**sacred** /ˈsā-krəd/ adjective: worthy of great respect or worship <example: a sacred duty>

was the specific question about what light would look that inspired him to write his famous book, "The Theory of Relativity." Indeed, many of the explanations in the book series stayed with him and later influenced Einstein's writing.

When Einstein was still in school at Luitpold Gymnasium, his father had to close his business. He and his business partner decided to try the same type of business in Milan, Italy. So, he moved the family there. However, Einstein stayed behind and lived in a boarding house in order to finish school.

Near the end of his school years, Einstein faced a hard decision. Einstein had become old enough that he faced what is called "**mandatory** military service" in Germany. He didn't want to serve in the military. So, he withdrew from school on a doctor's note, and left to join his family in Italy without completing school. He had to give up his status as a German citizen.

When he rejoined his family in Italy, his family was worried that he may face problems in the future because he had ended school early and avoided military service. Little did they know then who young Einstein would become!

---

mandatory /ˈman-də-ˌtȯr-ē/ adjective: required by law or by a rule <example: mandatory service>

CHAPTER 1
FUN FACTS

1. Albert Einstein was born in the German Empire. The German Empire existed between 1871 and 1919.

2. As a boy, Einstein was shown a compass by his father at the age of five. He was fascinated by it. It is thought that this is what sparked his interest in physics.

3. IQ stands for Intelligence Quotient. It is a measure of intelligence given as a result of special testing. It is thought that $2/3$ of people who take the test would score between 85 and 115.

Einstein's IQ is thought to have been 160.

4. Mandatory military service is called conscription. This means that when men or men and women turn a certain age, (such as 18 years old) they must serve in the military. Conscription is not common in the world. Most countries do not require military service. Of the countries that do, only some require all people of a certain age to serve. Germany stopped having mandatory military service in 2011.

CHAPTER 2

FAMILY
MATTERS

Albert Einstein was born to parents named Hermann Einstein and Pauline Koch. Hermann was an electrical engineer who worked as a salesman. He owned a company named Elektrotechnische Fabrik J. Einstein & Cie that he ran with his brother. His company was an electrical equipment company that was successful because they earned a large contract in Germany for business. Unfortunately, they lost the contract when Einstein was still in school.

The brothers felt they should try to move their business to Italy, so Herman moved the family. Einstein stayed behind in Germany to continue school but joined them after some time. The business struggled in Italy and was closed after only a couple of years. Later, Herman opened a new business with another relative. It was more successful. Unfortunately, he passed away at the pretty young age of 55 in Italy.

Dad

Einstein's mother was Pauline. She was a stay-at-home mom. She was known to be a quiet and lovely lady who was interested in the arts. She was also a talented musician. She played the piano well. <u>Her interest in music influenced Einstein. Pauline encouraged him to learn the violin. So, Einstein started playing violin at the age of five</u>.

After Einstein's father died in Milan, Italy, Pauline lived in Germany with his **paternal** aunt. His mother lived with them for over a decade and then in 1914 moved in with her brother, Jakob Koch, in Zurich, Switzerland. During this time, she worked as a housekeeper. Einstein was mainly studying and working in Switzerland after his father's

---

paternal /pə-ˈtər-nᵊl/ adjective: related to the father *<example: paternal grandparent>*

death. Towards the very end of his mother's life until she passed away in 1920, she lived with Einstein in Switzerland.

Einstein had only one sister. She was born with the name Maria but was known as Maja. Maja lived without Einstein throughout their childhood and moved with her parents to Italy, when her father lost his business in Germany.

Maja studied **literature** in college and eventually received a PhD, which is a **doctorate** degree.

---

literature /ˈli-tə-rə-ˌchùr/ noun: published writing, especially that which is considered important or artistic <example: The class read classic literature.>

doctorate /ˈdäk-t(ə-)rət/ noun: the highest degree at an academic institution <example: He received his doctorate.>

This means she became an expert on the subject she studied. She worked as a teacher for some time. Maja got married to a man named Paul Winteler. Paul was actually the son of Einstein's schoolmaster in Switzerland. Maja and Paul never had children together. They lived for a while in Switzerland together, where the Einsteins had family and later settled.

Unfortunately, Maja and Paul struggled with money. After some years of struggling in Switzerland, they decided to move to Italy and buy a house there. Einstein by then was pretty successful and could afford to help his sister, so he bought the house for them.

Maja and Einstein remained close throughout their life. After Maja's husband died, she went to live with Einstein who then was living in the United States, in New Jersey. She spent the rest of her life living there with Einstein.

CHAPTER 2
FUN FACTS

1. Einstein received a PhD from the University of Zurich in Switzerland. The abbreviation PhD stands for Doctor of Philosophy. This is the degree for doctors of any subject except for medicine.

2. Switzerland is a small mountainous country in the middle of Europe. It is really a beautiful country! Another fun fact is it is home to a couple of the most expensive cities to live in in the world. Geneva and Zurich make it to the top ten most expensive cities list and

often the top five year after year!

3. Einstein's sister Maja received a PhD in Literature. Literature is a category of writing that is pretty big. It includes many types of writing from many centuries in history. The definition of literature usually includes any written work that is considered an art form.

CHAPTER 3
A UNIQUE EDUCATION

Einstein stopped attending high school before he finished. This was because his family had moved to Italy so that his father could find work and also because Einstein wanted to avoid mandatory military service. However, education was important to the family, so he continued school and attended college and beyond.

In order to get into college, Einstein was encouraged to take entrance exams. He scored so high in math and physics on the exams that he was allowed to enter into a great college as long as he took pre-college classes to make up for the high school he missed. He did that.

Einstein went to college at a university called the Swiss Federal Polytechnic Institute in Zurich, Switzerland. He was 17 years old when he began his studies there. He studied maths and physics.

During his studies, Einstein excelled, but he continued to show an **independent** side of himself.

---

independent /ˌin-də-ˈpen-dənt/ adjective: not dependent or in control of by others *<example: independent of his parents>*

Sometimes he didn't show up for class and this bothered his teachers. Einstein didn't skip his classes to have fun. He was very serious about studying and loved learning. He just liked to learn on his own. He spent the time outside of class studying independently.

Einstein graduated from the Institute in 1900. He then went on to study at the University of Zurich in Switzerland. He graduated from his second university in 1905 with a PhD.

CHAPTER 3
FUN FACTS

1. The University of Zurich where Einstein received his PhD is in Switzerland. It was founded in 1833.

2. A few of the buildings that are part of the University of Zurich were originally part of an older school called Carolinum Zurich. Carolinum was a school that started in the same location in 1525. Can you believe it?

3. According to the Guinness Book of World Records, the world's oldest educational institution to give degrees out for study is the

University of Al Quaraouiyine in Fez, Morocco. Some might argue that this is not the oldest because the institution was focused on religious teaching. However, others argue that there were other subjects also taught. Morocco is a country in the north of Africa. The year this institution was founded was 859!

CHAPTER 4

A CAREER TO REMEMBER

Einstein graduated from Swiss Federal Polytechnic Institute in Zurich in the year 1900. He graduated with a teaching degree. Initially, he struggled to find a job. He had wanted to work as a teacher as his degree would suggest. Sometimes when students get to know their teachers and work hard in school, their teachers can help them find work after they graduate. However, Einstein had frequently skipped classes in order to work independently during his college years. Because of this, when the time came to find a job, he didn't find help from his teachers.

Patent Office

After a while, Einstein got his first job after graduating. It was not a teacher position as he had hoped. He found a job working in Switzerland at a patent office. A patent is a legal document that is awarded to an inventor for an invention. The patent is proof that the inventor made the invention, and it also gives the inventor all the rights and benefits of the invention.

Einstein's work at the patent office was good for two reasons. One reason is that the patents he reviewed for **approval** were related to electrical devices. You may remember that when Einstein was younger, he was fascinated by ideas about electricity. This job helped him develop his knowledge about electricity.

The second reason the job was good for Einstein was that it allowed him to continue with his independent studies. Einstein would

---

approval /ə-ˈprü-vəl/ noun: an act of affirming or accepting something <*example: Lily sought her parents' approval.*>

continue on to write many papers and books on math and physics and become very successful. This extra study time was important to him. Studying provided him with the knowledge he would later use to develop his ideas and write. It allowed him to develop some of his ideas that later he would turn into his published writing.

Miracle Year

Einstein's time at the patent office was so beneficial to his future career that one year there has been called his "miracle year." The year was 1905. During that year working at the patent office, Einstein wrote at least four major

groundbreaking papers that he later would become famous for.

The first paper was about how light works. Einstein used a theory that another **physicist** made to help explain a **phenomenon** known as photoelectric effect. "Photo" refers to light, so "photoelectric" effect refers to a light-electricity effect. Einstein noted in the paper that when light hits a material, the

groundbreaking /ˈgraủn(d)-ˌbrā-kiŋ/ adjective: fresh or new ideas *<example: a groundbreaking discovery>*

phenomenon /fi-ˈnä-mə-ˌnän/ noun 1: a rare fact or event 2: an observable fact or event *<example: an unusual phenomenon>*

physicist /ˈfi-zə-sist/ noun: a person trained in natural science *<example: She worked as a physicist.>*

material releases electrically charged particles. In Einstein's second paper he wrote about experiments that proved the existence of atoms. Einstein's third paper had a big and smart sounding name. The title was "On the Electrodynamics of Moving Bodies." It was a paper he became famous for.

In the paper, Einstein wrote about the theories of two famous scientists. He concluded that their theories **contradicted** each other.

---

atom /ˈa-təm/ noun: the smallest unit of an element that <example: a groundbreaking discovery>

contradict /ˌkän-trə-ˈdikt/ verb: to deny or imply the opposite of <example: Ann's actions contradicted her promises.>

That means, that if one was true, it was hard for the other to be true, and vice versa. Sir Isaac Newton and James Clerk Maxwell were the two scientists. Einstein used their theories and his thoughts about the issues with their theories to develop his own theory that famously became known as the theory of relativity. He introduced this theory in the paper.

Einstein's fourth paper that he wrote during his miracle year is the paper in which he wrote about his famous equation $E = mc^2$. Out loud this equation is read: E equals M C squared. This equation is about energy, mass and light.

Previously, energy and mass had been seen as unrelated. In this paper, Einstein wrote about how energy, mass and light are related to one another. The "C" in the equation refers to the constant speed of light.

Einstein continued to work at the patent office for a few years after his miracle year. It was an incredibly productive time for him! He finally stopped working there in 1909.

The University Professor

After finishing his work at the Swiss patent office, Einstein began his work as a university professor. He had wanted to teach at a university, but previously had a hard time finding a job as a professor at one. After his miracle year and getting his PhD, he finally got a job at the University of Zurich in Switzerland teaching full-time. He taught there for four years.

The Theory of Relativity

After teaching at the University of Zurich for a time, he got a job working at the University of Berlin in Germany. He was given the job of director of the Kaiser Wilhelm Institute for Physics. That may sound more complicated to you than it is! All that means is that he was put in charge of the physics institute at the University or Berlin.

While working as a director of the physics institute, Einstein wrote his masterwork, or his most famous paper on the general theory of relativity. He had only introduced his theory of relativity in one of his papers during his miracle year. This one was all about it. In Einstein's general theory of relativity, he found that gravity and motion can affect time and space. Now that sounds smart and complex!

This was the first time that gravity had been written about in 250 years, since Sir Isaac Newton wrote about it! It was so new and exciting that it really made headlines. It was written about in newspapers around the world. Newspapers called it a "Revolution in Science" and the "New Theory of the Universe." It really made Einstein's name famous.

Nobel Prize

Einstein's general theory of relativity made Einstein so famous that educators around the world asked Einstein to come and speak. Einstein toured around the world to places like Britain, France, Japan and the United States to talk about his ideas.

It was Einstein's theory of relativity that made Einstein famous, but it was one of his other theories that won him one of the biggest awards that any scientist can win, the Nobel Prize. Have you heard of the Nobel Prize? It is a big deal! It may have been the fame from his theory of relativity that got him noticed enough that he won this award, but it was too

controversial, so he did not win the award for it. He won the Nobel Prize in 1921 for his idea about the photoelectric effect.

Cosmology

Einstein built on his theories and developed a field of study called Cosmology. You may have heard many words with the suffix, or ending, -logy. If you see this ending in words, it means "the study of." It is an ending that is used commonly in English that is taken from an old Greek word "logia." The first part of the word is taken from the old Greek word

---

controversial /ˌkän-trə-ˈvər-shəl/ adjective: related to or causing disagreement or argument *<example: a controversial decision>*

"Kosmos." Cosmos refers to the universe. Cosmology is basically the study of the universe. Einstein isn't the first person to use the term cosmology, but he is generally believed to be the first person to start modern cosmology.

Hitler and the Nazi Party

You may have heard of a man named Adolf Hitler who once led Germany as chancellor, which is another word for the leader of a country, like a president or prime minister is. Well, Germany started facing some money difficulties in the 1920s after the Great War called World War I. The situation there became complicated.

Hitler joined a political party in Germany that would become known as the Nazi Party. He started his rise to power in the 1920s with the Nazi party and became the leader. The Nazi Party was becoming popular in Germany. They had negative things to say about certain types of people and especially Jews.

As you may recall, Einstein and his family were Jewish. It was not nice for Einstein to hear the talks of Hitler. Also, Einstein was a pacifist, which means he believed in peace and was against war. When Hitler and the Nazi Party started to become popular, Einstein looked to leave.

It became tense before he left. The Nazi Party was calling for

Jewish people to stop holding important jobs. Einstein became targeted directly before he left.

Einstein escaped Germany safely, and fled to Belgium, a nearby country in Europe. He left in 1932, one month before Hitler became leader of Germany. He later fled to England.

In England, Einstein was safe. However, he felt concerned when he thought about the many other professionals such as scientists and teachers in Germany that were Jewish and were being targeted by Hitler and the Nazi Party. He didn't want to leave them all behind stuck in Germany to possibly die like he may have if he hadn't escaped.

Tragically, the Nazis were no longer just saying terrible things about Jewish people. They were doing very bad, unthinkable things to Jewish people and also teachers and scientists.

Luckily, Einstein was introduced to Winston Churchill, who later became the leader of England. Winston Churchill helped many professors leave Germany and get jobs in Europe. Einstein also reached out to leaders in a country called Turkey. They also helped Jewish professionals leave and find jobs in other countries.

These actions saved lives. It is **estimated** that altogether the

---

estimate /'e-stə-ˌmāt/ verb: to guess at the size, value or nature of something *<example: He estimated the diamond's value.>* noun: a nonspecific calculation>

efforts of Einstein, with the help of the leaders of these countries, helped save the lives of around 1,000 people. This is truly one of the most amazing things that Einstein did in his life and showed that he was a **compassionate** man.

Einstein ended up leaving England and heading to the United States. He remained living there for the rest of his life. He never again returned to his birthplace, Germany.

The United States

Einstein fled Germany in 1932

---

compassionate /kəm-'pa-sh(ə-)nət/ adjective: showing sympathy *<example: a compassionate mother>*

and took a position at Princeton University in New Jersey at a newly formed institute called the Institute for Advanced Study.

Einstein was always an independent thinker. He became quite independent during his later years. Many of his fellow physicists and other scientists were focused on developing a theory called "quantum theory." Einstein went in his own direction.

During his later years working in Princeton, he continued to focus on his theories and tried to develop a **unified** theory that tied together many ideas. This unified theory is sometimes referred to as Einstein's

---

unified /ˈyü-nə-ˌfīd/ adjective: combined as one *<example: They were a unified team.>*

"Theory of Everything." The Theory of Everything was an attempt to explain the nature of all matter and energy in the universe. Now that is a big goal!

Unfortunately, Einstein was never able to finish his Theory of Everything. He wrote about it in 1950 in a magazine called Scientific American. He passed away five years later having not completed his work.

In the years after his death many of Einstein's ideas were confirmed. There were also new discoveries that helped develop what he was working on with his Theory of Everything, as well. Einstein's work continued to impress scientists and he became more and more famous and respected for his thinking and many groundbreaking ideas.

CHAPTER 4
FUN FACTS

1. Einstein is thought to have started modern Cosmology, which is the study of the universe. In the entire universe there are more stars than there are grains of sand in all the beaches of the world.

2. Cosmology is similar to astronomy. Both involve the study of the universe. However, cosmology involves the study of how the universe came to be and how it developed over time. Astronomy involves the studies of the parts of the

universe.

3. The universe is thought to be 13.7 billion years old. It is always growing in size and getting   bigger.

4. The Earth, if it were cloned, could fit into the sun over one million times – about 1 million!

5. The Earth is around 4.5 billion years old!

CHAPTER 5

HOBBIES AND PASSIONS

Einstein spent most of his life studying, working, and writing about his work. Interestingly, it was his hobbies that would bring him the most joy in life, so it has been said.

One of Einstein's hobbies was playing the violin. Einstein's mother introduced to the violin when he was a boy. He took lessons and played as a boy. He wasn't as interested in violin at a young age as he was later on, partly because he had to develop the skill first. He did slowly though, and afterwards he was so grateful to be able to play. Playing the violin was something that brought him joy and he continued to play until a few years before he died.

Another hobby of Einstein's was listening to music. This was actually his favorite! He loved listening to music! He first was introduced to music at a young age, when he heard the music of Mozart, who was a classical composer from the 1700s. Einstein is said to have noted once that music is what had brought him the most joy in life.

A third big hobby of Einstein's was sailing. Being on the water and sailing was a way that Einstein was able to relax and unwind after all the hard work and thinking he did so much. It is important we all find healthy ways to relax after stressful tasks!

Einstein wasn't such a great sailor. He had a hard time steering it sometimes. It doesn't matter, though, because he loved sailing anyway. You do not have to be good at something in order to enjoy it!

Einstein received a sailboat in his fifties from friends. He gave the sailboat a name. Can you guess the sailboat's name? It is a German word. The name was Tuemmler. A

Tuemmler in German is a bottlenose dolphin.

CHAPTER 5
FUN FACTS

1. Einstein played the violin. The violin is a string instrument. The violin is known to be first created and used in Italy in the 1600s.

2. Mozart was one of Einstein's favorite composers. Mozart lived from 1756 -1791. He was born in Austria.

3. Mozart's full birth name was Wolfgang Amadeus Mozart.

4. Einstein loved to sail. The expression "feeling blue" comes from sailing. In the past, when sailors experienced

someone dying on board, they would raise a blue flag on the ship.

CHAPTER 6
A PERSONAL LIFE

Einstein was married two times and also had three children. He met his first wife when he was in college at the Swiss Federal Polytechnic Institute in Zurich, Switzerland. Her name was Mileva Marić. She was from a country in Europe called Serbia. Einstein and Mileva first became great friends who spent a lot of time studying together. They would spend many hours discussing math and physics theories. Many people believe that it was these discussions that were critical in Einstein later developing the ones he became famous for.

Before they were married, Einstein and Mileva had a baby girl named Lieserl. At some point early in Lieserl's life, Mileva travelled to Serbia to visit family. She later returned to Switzerland without the baby. There is no record of what happened to little Lierserl. However, at the time, it was not common for a couple to have a baby without being married. It is possible that the little girl was secretly adopted. It is also possible that the little girl died as a baby of scarlet fever.

In 1903, Mileva and Einstein married. They had a second child in 1904 named Hans Albert Einstein and a third in 1910 named Eduard. Einstein and Meliva stayed married until 1919, but they separated and lived in different cities starting five years earlier. It seems that Einstein had fallen out of love. However, Einstein wanted to take care of Mileva after they divorced, so he offered her to have all of his future Nobel Prize money.

Einstein fell in love with another woman named Elsa Lowenthal. They married in 1919. They did not have any children together. They remained married until Elsa passed away in 1936.

One of Einstein's children, his youngest, Eduard, grew up and became a doctor of psychiatry. Unfortunately, his story turned tragic, and he was diagnosed with a mental illness called schizophrenia. He lost his ability to work after some time. HIs mother cared for him until she died. After that he lived in a hospital where he received mental care. That is where he lived until he died in 1965. When Einstein moved to the United States, he was unable to see his son again, but they kept in contact through letters until Einstein died in 1955.

Einstein's second child, Hans Albert, grew up to be an engineer and professor who lived and taught in the United States. He taught engineering for a long time at the University of California,

Berkeley, in San Francisco. He had three biological children named Bernhard, Klaus, and David and one adopted named Evelyn. Sadly, two of his biological children passed away during childhood.

Bernhard Cesar Einstein is the only biological grandchild of Einstein known to have survived into adulthood. He had five children, all of whom are alive as of 2022 and are direct **descendants** of Albert Einstein. Three of them were born in the United States.

---

descendant /di-'sen-dənt/ noun: moving downward from an ancestor or source *<example: His ancestors came from Poland.>*

ADAM KENT

CHAPTER 6
FUN FACTS

1. In families, an ancestor is who you came from. The study of your family history is called genealogy.

2. Albert Einstein has living relatives. He has two living grandkids. He has five living great grandkids. That makes Albert Einstein their ancestor.

3. It is thought that Einstein's first daughter may have passed away when she was just a baby from scarlet fever. Scarlet fever is an illness that used to be feared but is no

longer. In the past, before we had antibiotics and other treatments for it, many people died from it. However, today it is easily treated! It is also much less common.

CHAPTER 7

A LASTING LEGACY

Albert Einstein's lasting legacy is like a shining star in the sky. He was a brilliant scientist who changed the way we think about the universe. Through his clever ideas and mind-bending equations, he showed us that even the smallest atom can hold tremendous power.

Einstein's most famous equation, $E=mc^2$, taught us that energy and matter are deeply connected. This discovery has led to amazing inventions and incredible feats in science, like the creation of nuclear energy. He helped us understand that the universe is like a giant puzzle, and with every discovery we make, we get closer to understanding its secrets.

But Einstein's legacy goes beyond science. He was a man of peace and understanding, who spoke up against injustice and fought for a world where everyone is treated with kindness and respect.

So, remember the amazing legacy of Albert Einstein. Let his curiosity and creativity ignite your own passion for learning. Dream big, explore the wonders of the universe, and always remember that you too can make a difference, just like this extraordinary man who changed the world with his genius and his heart.

INSPIRATIONAL QUOTES

Quotes are like magical words that can lift your spirits and make you feel like you can conquer the world! They are short and powerful sentences that carry big messages. Quotes come from inspiring people who have experienced many things in life. They teach us valuable lessons, remind us to be brave, and encourage us to follow our dreams.

So, whenever you need some inspiration or a little boost of confidence, just read a quote, and you'll feel like you can achieve anything! Here are a few quotes from Einstein to inspire you on your way!

" Learn from yesterday, live for today, hope for tomorrow: The important thing is not to stop questioning."

" Life is like a bicycle. To keep balance, you must keep moving."

" A person who never made a mistake never tried anything new."

" If you cannot explain it simply, you don't understand it enough."

" We cannot solve our problems with the same thinking we used when we created them."

" The only source of knowledge is experience."

" Peace cannot be kept by force; it can only be achieved by understanding."

" There are two ways you can live: you can live as if nothing is a miracle; you can live as if everything is a miracle."

" Everything should be made as simple as possible, but not simpler."

" The gift of fantasy has meant more to me than my talent for absorbing positive knowledge."

" Try not to become a man of success but rather a man of value."

" The world is a dangerous place to live; not because of the people who are evil, but because of the people who don't do anything about it."

"
The difference between stupidity and genius is that genius has its limits."

"
In the middle of difficulty lies opportunity."

"
The measure of intelligence is the ability to change."

"   Education is what remains after one has forgotten what one has learned in school."

"   Reality is merely an illusion, albeit a very persistent one."

"   Strive not to be a success, but rather to be of value."

"   The true sign of intelligence is not knowledge but imagination."

" Insanity: doing the same thing over and over again and expecting different results."

BOOK
DISCUSSION

How do you think that Albert Einstein's upbringing contributed to her success?

_____
_____
_____
_____
_____
_____
_____
_____

What other factors do you think contributed to Einstein's success?

_____
_____
_____
_____
_____
_____

What are some qualities that you like about Einstein?

_____
_____
_____
_____
_____
_____
_____
_____

What would you guess is Einstein's favorite color and why?

_____
_____
_____
_____
_____
_____
_____
_____

What is your favorite inspirational quote by Albert Einstein and why?

_____
_____
_____
_____
_____
_____
_____
_____

GLOSSARY

approval /ə-'prü-vəl/ noun: an act of affirming or accepting something *<example: Lily sought her parents' approval.>*

atom /'a-təm/ noun: the smallest unit of an element that *<example: a groundbreaking discovery>*

compassionate /kəm-'pa-sh(ə)nət/ adjective: showing sympathy *<example: a compassionate mother>*

contradict /ˌkän-trə-'dikt/ verb: to deny or imply the opposite of *<example: Ann's actions contradicted her promises.>*

controversial /ˌkän-trə-'vər-shəl/ adjective: related to or causing disagreement or argument *<example: a controversial decision>*

descendant /di-'sen-dənt/ noun: moving downward from an ancestor or source *<example: His ancestors came from Poland.>*

doctorate /'däk-t(ə-)rət/ noun: the highest degree at an academic institution *<example: He received his doctorate.>*

estimate /'e-stə-ˌmāt/ verb: to guess at the size, value or nature of something *<example: He estimated the diamond's value.>*

noun: a nonspecific calculation>

fascinate /ˈfa-sə-ˌnāt/ verb: to hold the interest of in a powerful way *<example: The acrobat's performance fascinated her.>*

groundbreaking /ˈgraủn(d)-ˌbrā-kiŋ/ adjective: fresh or new ideas *<example: a groundbreaking discovery>*

independent /ˌin-də-ˈpen-dənt/ adjective: not dependent or in control of by others *<example: independent of his parents>*

influence /ˈin-ˌflü-ən(t)s/ noun: the power to cause an effect in an indirect way verb: to affect or change indirectly *<example: His teacher influenced him.>*

literature /ˈli-tə-rə-ˌchu̇r/ noun: published writing, especially that which is considered important or artistic *<example: The class read classic literature.>*

mandatory /ˈman-də-ˌtȯr-ē/ adjective: required by law or by a rule *<example: mandatory service>*

paternal /pə-ˈtər-nᵊl/ adjective: related to the father *<example: paternal grandparent>*

phenomenon /fi-ˈnä-mə-ˌnän/ noun 1: a rare fact or event 2: an observable fact or event *<example: an unusual phenomenon>*

physicist /'fi-zə-sist/ noun: a person trained in natural science *<example: She worked as a physicist.>*

sacred /'sā-krəd/ adjective: worthy of great respect or worship *<example: a sacred duty>*

unified /'yü-nə-ˌfīd/ adjective: combined as one *<example: They were a unified team.>*

SELECTED REFERENCES

"Albert Einstein – Biography". Nobel Foundation. 6 March 2007.

"Albert Einstein Quits Germany, Renounces Citizenship". *History Unfolded: US Newspapers and the Holocaust.* 17 April 2021.

"Albert Einstein (1879–1955)". Royal Netherlands Academy of Arts and Sciences. 23 September 2015.

Albert Einstein. (4 April 2018). Retrieved from https://www.biography.com/scientist/albert-einstein

"A New Physics, Based on Einstein". *The New York Times*. 25 November 1919. p. 17. 8 June 2019.

Braaten, Ellen B.; Norman, Dennis (1 November 2006). "Intelligence (IQ) Testing". *Pediatrics in Review*. 27 (11): 403–408.

Bodanis, David (2000). *$E = mc^2$: A Biography of the World's Most Famous Equation*. New York: Walker.

Costliest cities in the world. (January 2022) https://en.wikipedia.org/wiki/Costliest_cities_in_the_world

"Einstein and his love of music" (PDF). Physics World. January 2005.

"Einstein at the patent office" (official website). Berne, Switzerland: Swiss Federal Institute of Intellectual Property, IGE/IPI. 6 February 2014. 30 August 2016.

"FAQ about Einstein and the Institute" (official website). Berne, Switzerland: Swiss Federal Institute of Intellectual Property, IGE/IPI. 27 May 2014. 12 June 2021.

"Getting up close and personal with Einstein". *The Jerusalem Post* /

JPost.com. 23 September 2020.

Golden, Frederic (3 January 2000). "Person of the Century: Albert Einstein". *Time.* 21 February 2006.

Halpern, Paul (2019). "Albert Einstein, celebrity scientist". *Physics Today.* 72 (4): 38–45. 14 April 2021.

Heilbron, John L., ed. (2003). *The Oxford Companion to the History of Modern Science.* Oxford University Press. p. 233. 27 November 2016.

Hoffmann, Dieter (2013). *Einstein's Berlin: In the footsteps of a genius*. Baltimore: The Johns Hopkins University Press. pp. 2-9, 28.

Hoffman, Miles (1997). *The NPR Classical Music Companion: Terms and Concepts from A to Z*. Houghton Mifflin Harcourt.

"How Einstein fled from the Nazis to an Oxford college". *The Oxford Times*. 2012. 2 April 2015.

"Introduction: Cosmology – space". *New Scientist*. 4 September 2006.

List of Best-Selling Books. (13 June 2022.)

https://en.wikipedia.org/wiki/List_of_best-selling_books

May, Andrew (2017). Clegg, Brian (ed.). *Albert Einstein, in 30-Second Physics: The 50 most fundamental concepts in physics, each explained in half a minute*. London: Ivy Press. pp. 108–109.

Missner, Marshall (May 1985). "Why Einstein Became Famous in America". *Social Studies of Science*. 15 (2): 267–291.

The 10 Oldest Universities in the World. (Date estimated to be in 2019.) https://www.oldest.org/culture/universities/

"On His 135th Birthday, Einstein is Still Full of Surprises". *Out There*. 14 March 2014. 18 March 2014.

Overbye, Dennis (24 November 2015). "A Century Ago, Einstein's Theory of Relativity Changed Everything". *The New York Times*. 1 January 2022.

Overbye, Dennis (17 April 2017). "'Genius' Unravels the Mysteries of Einstein's Universe". *The New York Times*. 18 April 2017.

Pais, Abraham (October 1979). "Einstein and the quantum theory" (PDF). *Reviews of*

Modern Physics. 51 (4): 863–914.

Peter Galison; Gerald James Holton; Silvan S. Schweber (2008). *Einstein for the 21st Century: His Legacy in Science, Art, and Modern Culture.* Princeton University Press. pp. 161–164.

Richard Kroehling (July 1991). "Albert Einstein: How I See the World". *American Masters.* PBS. 14 November 2011.

Robinson, Andrew (2015). *Einstein: A Hundred Years of Relativity.* Princeton University Press. pp. 143–145. 27 November 2016.

Rosenkranz, Ze'ev (6 November 2002). *The Einstein Scrapbook*. Baltimore, Maryland: Johns Hopkins University Press.

Rowe, David E.; Schulmann, Robert (8 June 2007a). David A., Walsh (ed.). "What Were Einstein's Politics?". *History News Network*. 3 February 2019.

Universe Facts. (Date unknown.) https://www.natgeokids.com/uk/discover/science/space/universe-facts/

"The University of Zurich – At a Glance". University of Zurich. 2020.

"Volume 9: The Berlin Years: Correspondence, January 1919 – April 1920 (English translation supplement) page 6". *einsteinpapers.press.princeton.edu*. 4 October 2021.

Whittaker, E. (1 November 1955). "Albert Einstein. 1879–1955". *Biographical Memoirs of Fellows of the Royal Society*. 1: 37–67.

"The World Factbook: Military service age and obligation". CIA. 22 March 2016.

LETTER FROM THE AUTHOR

Dear Readers,

I hope you enjoyed this book and learned some take away that may help you as you continue to grow and make choices in life. Reading biographies of famous people can help us learn about ourselves and what decisions help and hurt people as they follow their dreams. If you enjoyed learning about this icon, you can read about more in our kids biographies series!

Happy learning and may your dreams come true!

All the best,

Adam Kent

COLLECT THE WHOLE *GET SMART* BOOK SERIES

Here are just a few:

Join our book club for free book offers. For more info email:

info@rocketkidsbookclub.com

Made in the USA
Las Vegas, NV
26 February 2024